A Book About YOU
Written by Me!

Written by Linda Schwartz • Illustrated by Bev Armstrong • Cover by Lucyna A. M. Green

The Learning Works

Editing and Text Design: Kimberley A. Clark
Cover Art: Lucyna A. M. Green

Copyright © 1998
Creative Teaching Press, Inc.
Huntington Beach, CA 92649

ISBN: 0-88160-320-1
LW 383

Printed in the United States of America.

From Me to You

To _____

Paste your photo here and fill
in your name on the line below.

From _____

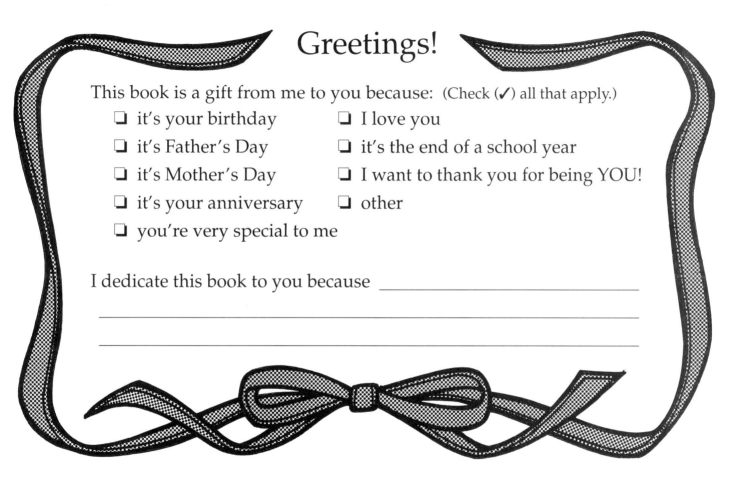

Greetings!

This book is a gift from me to you because: (Check (✔) all that apply.)

❏ it's your birthday ❏ I love you

❏ it's Father's Day ❏ it's the end of a school year

❏ it's Mother's Day ❏ I want to thank you for being YOU!

❏ it's your anniversary ❏ other

❏ you're very special to me

I dedicate this book to you because _____

_____

_____

A Checklist of You

Check the best answers . . .

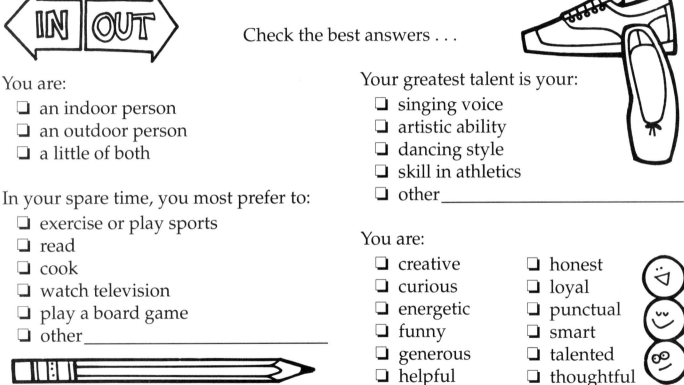

You are:
- ❏ an indoor person
- ❏ an outdoor person
- ❏ a little of both

In your spare time, you most prefer to:
- ❏ exercise or play sports
- ❏ read
- ❏ cook
- ❏ watch television
- ❏ play a board game
- ❏ other_____

Your greatest talent is your:
- ❏ singing voice
- ❏ artistic ability
- ❏ dancing style
- ❏ skill in athletics
- ❏ other_____

You are:
- ❏ creative
- ❏ curious
- ❏ energetic
- ❏ funny
- ❏ generous
- ❏ helpful
- ❏ honest
- ❏ loyal
- ❏ punctual
- ❏ smart
- ❏ talented
- ❏ thoughtful

Your Favorite Things

I think these are your favorites:

actor _____   movie _____

actress _____   place to shop _____

book _____   place to visit _____

color _____   restaurant _____

food _____   song _____

game _____   sport _____

hobby _____   television show _____

holiday _____   thing to wear _____

ice cream _____   time of day _____

About You

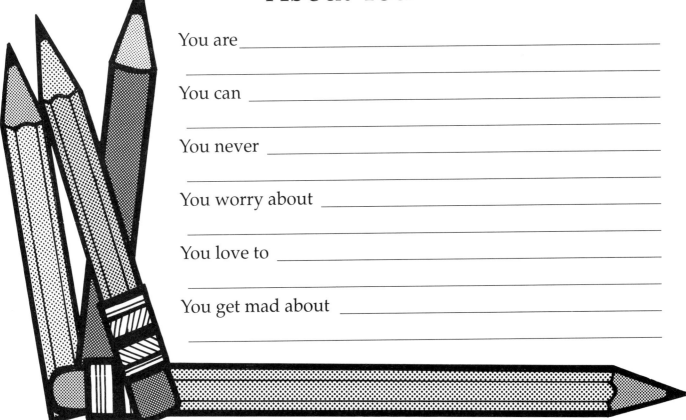

You are _____

_____

You can _____

_____

You never _____

_____

You worry about _____

_____

You love to _____

_____

You get mad about _____

_____

About You

You sometimes _____

_____

You think _____

_____

You are crazy about _____

_____

You don't like to _____

_____

You and I enjoy _____

_____

You're a whiz at_____

_____

When I Think of You

Here is a picture, symbol, or drawing of something that comes to mind when I think of you.

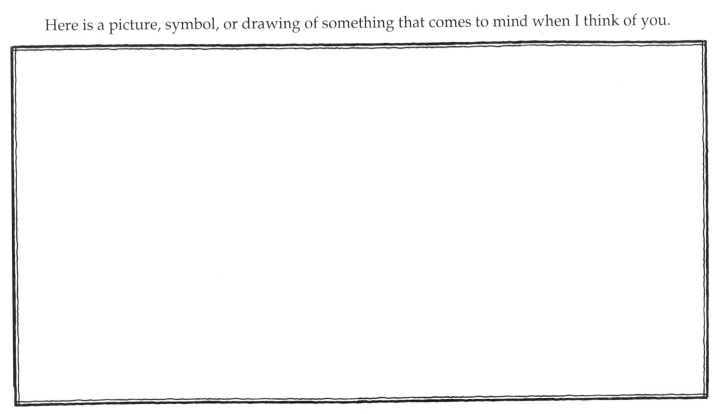

You Are Special

Here are three reasons why you are special to me.

1. _____
   _____
   _____

2. _____
   _____
   _____

3. _____
   _____
   _____

Memories

I'll never forget the time you _____

_____

_____

_____

Something funny that happened to us was when _____

_____

_____

_____

Memories

One of the nicest things you ever did for me was _____

_____

_____

_____

A great time we had together was _____

_____

_____

_____

A T for You

Here is a t-shirt
I designed for you.

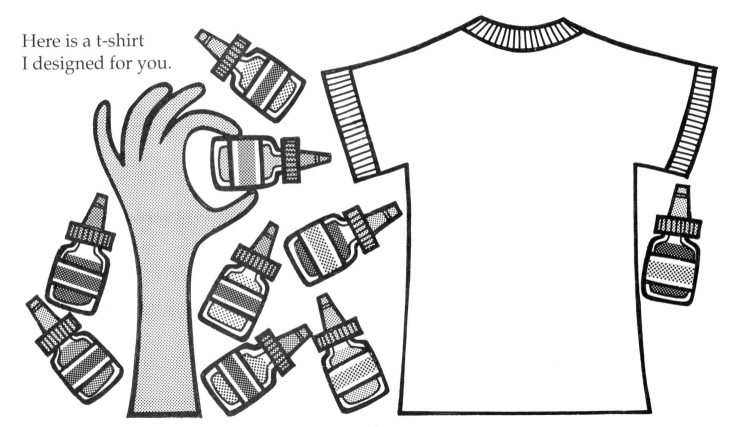

Bumper Sticker

Here is a bumper sticker I designed for you.

ASK ME ABOUT MY MODEL TRAINS

I ♥ ⚾

I BRAKE FOR CHOCOLATE!

Special You

I think you're great at _____

_____

One thing you've done that I admire is _____

_____

You are happiest when _____

_____

You have taught me to _____

_____

Special You

I liked when you _____

_____

I appreciate your _____

_____

You saved the day when you _____

_____

You are famous for _____

_____

Coupons for You

This coupon is good for _____

_____

_____

_____

This coupon is good for _____

_____

_____

_____

This coupon is good for _____

_____

_____

_____

Coupons for You

This coupon is good for _____

_____

_____

_____

This coupon is good for _____

_____

_____

_____

This coupon is good for _____

_____

_____

_____

Your Life Story

Here is a book jacket that I designed for a story about your life.

If You Were President

If you were president of the United States, you would probably _____

_____

_____

_____

_____

_____

_____

_____

_____

_____

_____

_____

My Poem for You

Here is a poem I've written just for you.

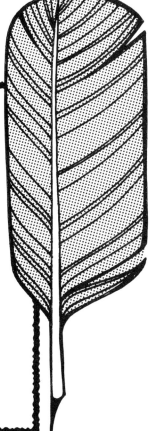

Two Wishes

If I could have any two wishes come true for you, I would wish

E-Mail From Me

If . . .

If you were a vehicle, I think you would be
a/an _____
because _____
_____

If you were an animal, I think you would be
a/an _____
because _____
_____

23

A Lot Alike

You and I have many things in common.
Here are some ways I'm glad we are alike:

_____

_____

_____

_____

_____

_____

_____

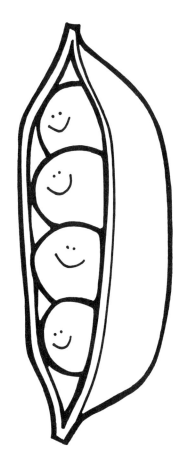

_____

_____

_____

Definitely Different

Being different makes things interesting!
Here are some ways you and I are *not* alike.

_____

_____

_____

_____

_____

_____

_____

_____

_____

A Gift for You

If I could give you anything in the world, I would give you _____ .
Here's a picture of your gift.

A Movie About You

If I were making a movie about your life, I would choose

_____ to play the part of you.
actor/actress

The supporting roles of _____ and

_____ would be played by

_____ and _____ .
actor/actress   actor/actress

A good choice for director would be _____ .
director

The movie would be filmed in _____
location

and would be called _____ .
title

A Movie About You

Here is a scene from the movie about your life.

What's Cooking?

If I were cooking a special meal for you, here's what would be on the menu.

appetizer _____

main course _____

_____

vegetable _____

salad _____

dessert _____

drink _____

Read All About You

You made the front page headline! Here's what the newspaper says about YOU!

your picture

28-Hour Day

If there were four extra hours in a day, here is how I would spend them with you.

_____

_____

_____

_____

_____

_____

_____

_____

_____

_____

Your Future

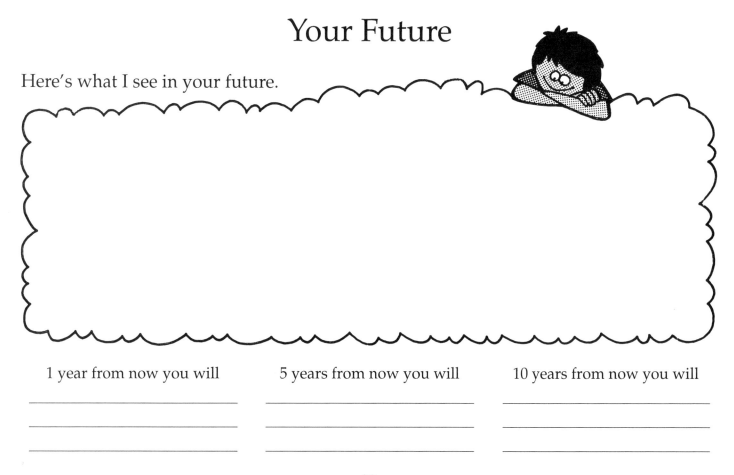

Here's what I see in your future.

1 year from now you will

_____

_____

_____

5 years from now you will

_____

_____

_____

10 years from now you will

_____

_____

_____